Sept 1

To W___,

Love You

Jackie
&
Knobby

Happy Birthday!!

Heaven on Earth

The Inspirational Writings
Of Saint Francis of Assisi

Heaven on Earth

Selected by Karen Hill
Illustrated by
Noreen Bonker

HALLMARK EDITIONS

HEAVEN ON EARTH

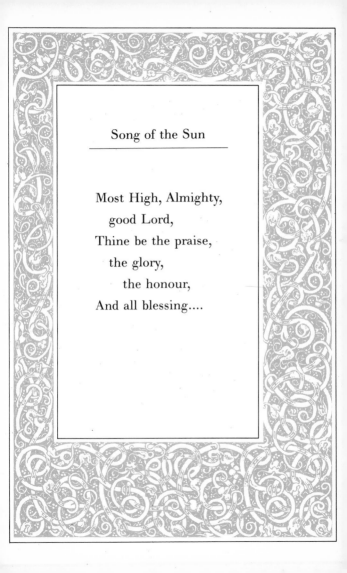

Song of the Sun

Most High, Almighty,
 good Lord,
Thine be the praise,
 the glory,
  the honour,
And all blessing....

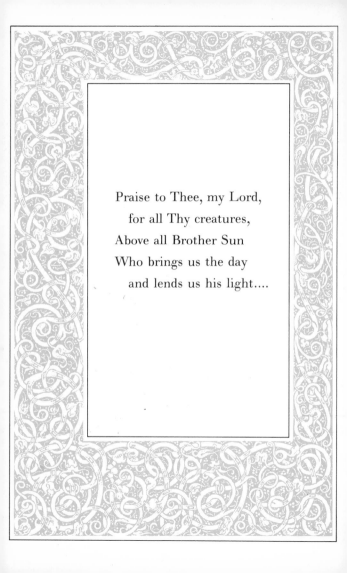

Praise to Thee, my Lord,
for all Thy creatures,
Above all Brother Sun
Who brings us the day
and lends us his light....

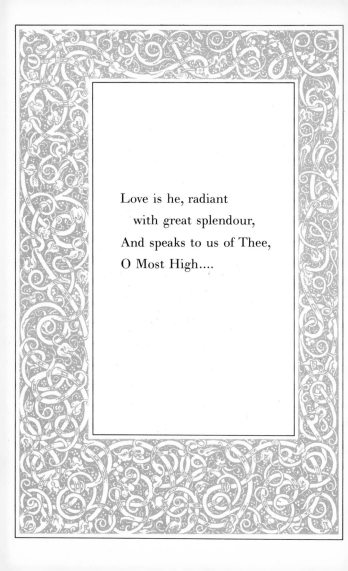

Love is he, radiant
  with great splendour,
And speaks to us of Thee,
O Most High....

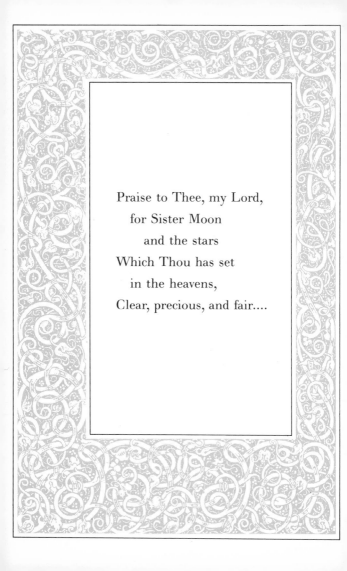

Praise to Thee, my Lord,
for Sister Moon
and the stars
Which Thou has set
in the heavens,
Clear, precious, and fair....

Praise to Thee, my Lord,
 for Brother Wind,
For air and cloud,
 for calm and all weather,
By which Thou
 supportest life
  in all Thy creatures....

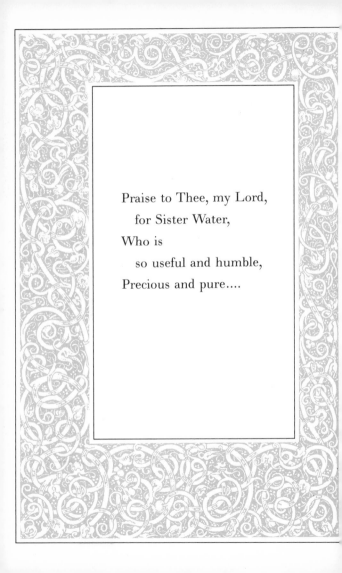

Praise to Thee, my Lord,
  for Sister Water,
Who is
  so useful and humble,
Precious and pure....

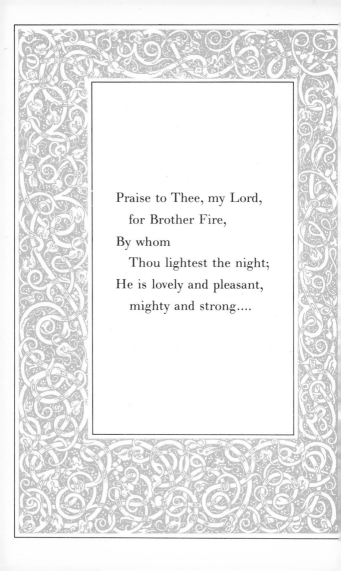

Praise to Thee, my Lord,
   for Brother Fire,
By whom
   Thou lightest the night;
He is lovely and pleasant,
   mighty and strong....

Praise to Thee, my Lord,
  for our sister
      Mother Earth
Who sustains
  and directs us,
And brings forth
  varied fruits
      and coloured flowers.

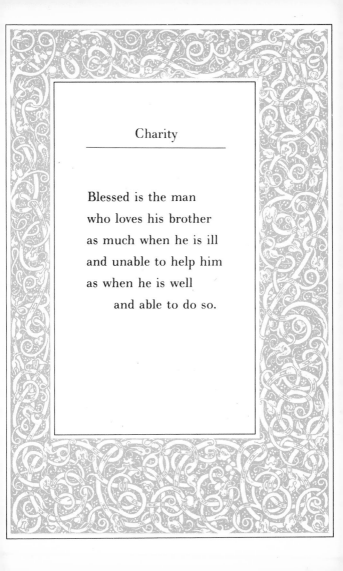

Charity

Blessed is the man
who loves his brother
as much when he is ill
and unable to help him
as when he is well
and able to do so.

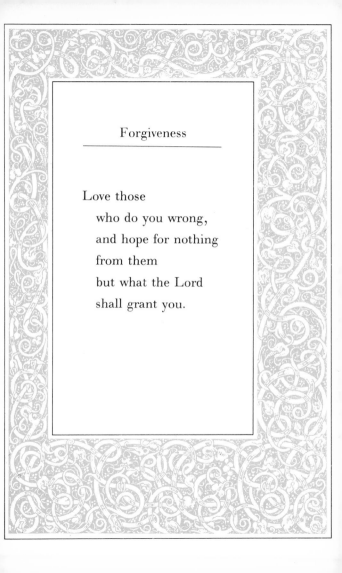

Forgiveness

Love those
who do you wrong,
and hope for nothing
from them
but what the Lord
shall grant you.

Song of Love

Where there is charity
and wisdom,
there is neither fear
nor ignorance....

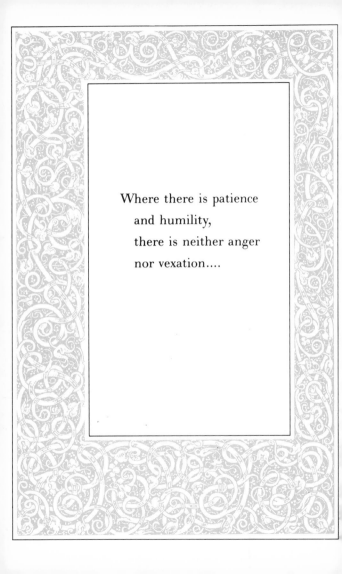

Where there is patience
and humility,
there is neither anger
nor vexation....

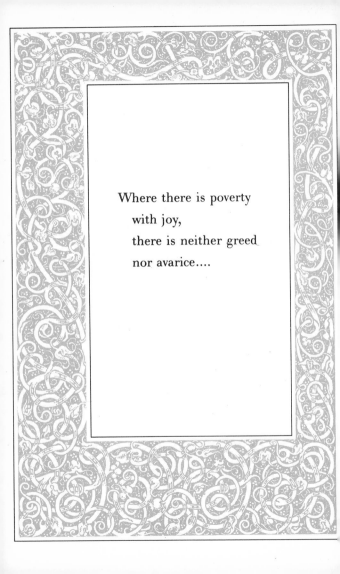

Where there is poverty
with joy,
there is neither greed
nor avarice....

Where there is peace
and meditation,
there is neither anxiety
nor doubt....

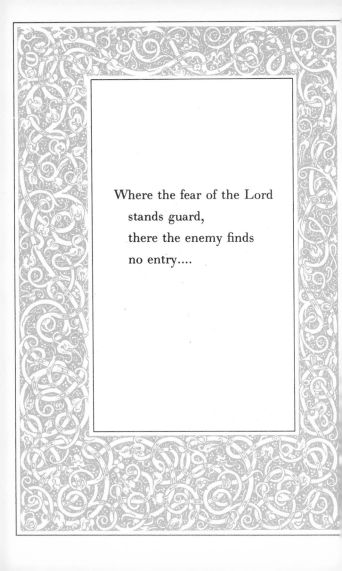

Where the fear of the Lord
stands guard,
there the enemy finds
no entry....

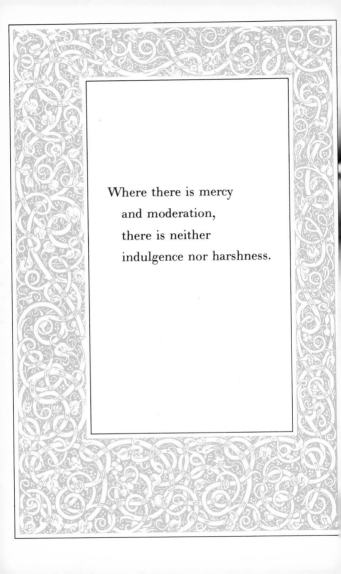

Where there is mercy
and moderation,
there is neither
indulgence nor harshness.

Friendship

Blessed is the man
  who helps his neighbour
  in trouble,
  just as
  he would wish
  to be helped in like
    circumstances.

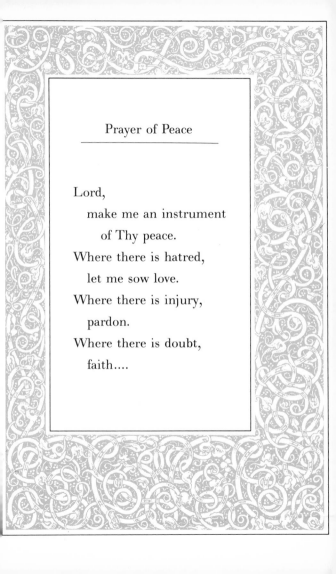

Prayer of Peace

Lord,
    make me an instrument
      of Thy peace.
Where there is hatred,
    let me sow love.
Where there is injury,
    pardon.
Where there is doubt,
    faith....

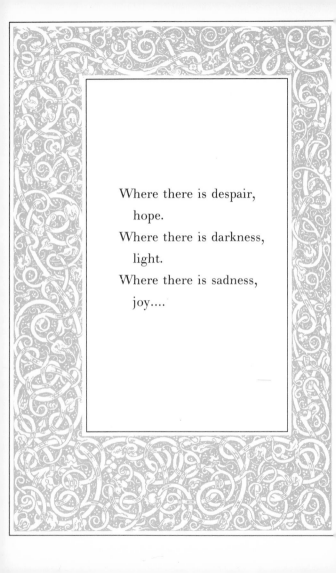

Where there is despair,
    hope.
Where there is darkness,
    light.
Where there is sadness,
    joy....

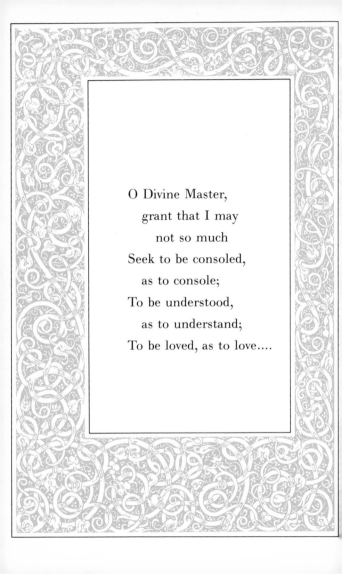

O Divine Master,
   grant that I may
      not so much
Seek to be consoled,
   as to console;
To be understood,
   as to understand;
To be loved, as to love....

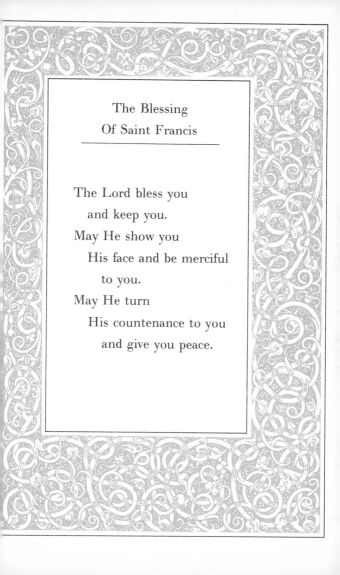

The Blessing
Of Saint Francis

The Lord bless you
 and keep you.
May He show you
 His face and be merciful
 to you.
May He turn
 His countenance to you
 and give you peace.